A Star in My Orange

Looking for Nature's Shapes

DANA MEACHEN RAU

Ⓜ MILLBROOK PRESS · MINNEAPOLIS

For all of my teachers, past and present, at school and at home.
D.M.R.

Cover photograph courtesy of © Maximilian Stock Ltd./Animals Animals/Earth Scenes

Photographs courtesy of Photo Researchers, Inc.: pp. 3 (©John Sanford/SPL), 13 (© G. C. Kelley), 18 (© Ken Cavanagh), 27 (© George Holton), 29 (NASA/SPL), 30 (top left © Rod Planck; bottom left © Francoise Sauze/SPL; bottom right © Jeff Lepore), 31 (top left © Joyce Photographics; top right © David Hall); Animals Animals/Earth Scenes: pp. 5 (© Maximilian Stock Ltd.), 6 (© Scott Smith), 10 (© Patti Murray), 24 (© Peter Weimann), 25 (© Ralph Reinhold); Bruce Coleman, Inc.: pp. 9 (© J. Shaw), 22 (© Jane Burton), 31 (center right © J. C. Carton; bottom left © C. C. Lockwood); PhotoEdit: p. 14 (© Myrleen Cate); © Wolfgang Kaehler 2000 www.wkaehlerphoto.com: pp. 17, 31 (bottom right); Minden Pictures: p. 21 (© Tim Fitzharris); Peter Arnold, Inc.: p. 30 (top right © Walter H. Hodge)

Millbrook Press
A division of Lerner Publishing Group, Inc.
241 First Avenue North
Minneapolis, Minnesota 55401 U.S.A.

Website address: www.lernerbooks.com

Library of Congress Cataloging-in-Publication Data
Rau, Dana Meachen, 1971-
A star in my orange / by Dana Meachen Rau.
p. cm.
Summary: Photographs and simple text explains how various shapes and patterns can be found all around in nature.
ISBN-13: 978-0-7613-2414-0 (lib. bdg. : alk. paper)
ISBN-10: 0-7613-2414-3 (lib. bdg. : alk. paper)
1. Geometry—Juvenile literature. 2. Geometry in nature—Juvenile literature.
[1. Shape.] I. Title.
QA445.5 .R38 2002   516—dc21   2001032696
Manufactured in the United States of America
3 4 5 6 7 8 — DP — 13 12 11 10 09 08

A star in the sky isn't the only star I can see.

There's a star inside my orange,

in a tide pool,

in a snowflake,

and in a daisy.

The antlers of a deer
look like branches on a tree.

My arms and my hands
look like branches, too.

I see lots of little shapes
in a turtle's shell,

and a bee's honeycomb,

and a fallen pinecone.

There are spinning spirals
everywhere I look.

A seahorse is curvy.

A ram's horns are twirly.

A pig's tail is curly.

A shell's shape is swirly.

Spirals are making me dizzy!

I'm spinning,
just like the Earth through
the sky of stars.

BLUEBERRIES

Nature is full of different patterns. You can find them almost everywhere you look. The next time you go outside, or even to the grocery store, search for stars, spirals, branches, and little repeated shapes.

A STAR FRU

Now that you have peeked inside an orange to see a star, look inside lemons, apples, and grapefruits, too. The top of blueberries and the leaves on eggplants and tomatoes also have star shapes. There is even a fruit called a starfruit—each slice is shaped like a star. Have you ever studied the underside of a mushroom? The gills that come out from the center look like a starburst. So do the petals of many flowers, such as mums and lilies.

You can find spinning spirals at the beach when you watch the water. Waves curl in a spiral shape before they splash onto the shore. A whirlpool of water has a spiral shape. Spirals are also found on some plants, such as the long curls called tendrils that grow on grapevines. Even millipedes sometimes curl themselves up in a spiral shape.

A WHIRLPOOL

A MILLIPEDE

A PINEAPPLE

A SEA SPONGE

Many foods have little repeated shapes. The skin of a pineapple has lots of little shapes. So do raspberries and blackberries, strawberries, artichokes, corn, and peanut shells. Animals often have little shapes, too. Have you ever seen an armadillo's shell? A sea sponge? Coral? A fish's scales? The eyes of a fly and the wings of a dragonfly are also made up of lots of little shapes.

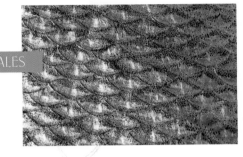

FISH SCALES

Branching is not only found on a tree's branches. Its roots also look like branches. Peer closely at a tree's leaves and you'll see a branching pattern as well. Feathers on a bird are like branches. Even big things in nature show branching, such as a large river and the smaller rivers that flow into it. There are branches inside you, too. The veins and arteries that bring blood around your body look like branches.

PEACOCK FEATHERS

RIVERS

About the Author

Dana Meachen Rau loves to explore nature. When she was a child, she helped her father feed the birds and took nature walks with her mother. She and her brother dug in dirt and climbed in trees. Together, her family planted gardens.

Today, Dana plants gardens with her husband, Chris, and son, Charlie. Charlie has just learned his shapes and looks for them everywhere—in flowers, on bugs, and even in puddles. Dana is the author of more than fifty books for children. She is also an editor and illustrator, and works from her home office in Farmington, Connecticut.